Not Only Journals VIP Club

Join our **VIP Club** where we'll notify you anytime there is a special offer. Visit the link below, put your email in the box and you will be the first to know of our new releases, freebies, discounts and giveaways.

http://NotOnlyJournals.com/VIPaccess/

CPSIA information can be obtained
at www.ICGtesting.com
Printed in the USA
LVHW082109021218
599022LV00018B/348/P